ART FOR CONSERVATION

THE FEDERAL DUCK STAMPS

Art for Conservation
The Federal Duck Stamps

by Jene C. Gilmore

INTRODUCTION BY
ROBERT HINES

BARRE PUBLISHERS 1971 BARRE, MASSACHUSETTS

Copyright © 1971 by Barre Publishing Co., Inc.
Library of Congress Catalog Card No. 78-163882
ISBN 8271-7122-6
All rights reserved
Designed by Klaus Gemming, New Haven, Connecticut
Composed by Finn Typographic Service, Inc., Stamford, Connecticut
Printed by The Meriden Gravure Company, Meriden, Connecticut
Bound by A. Horowitz & Son, Clifton, New Jersey
Manufactured in the United States of America

Acknowledgments

No BOOK which requires research and documentation for its success can be done without the cooperation of many people. This book is no exception.

For their part I'd like to thank the following: Gilbert Verney, for the loan of twelve prints from his fine collection; Dr. Shepherd Kreech, whose diary really started this book; Mrs. A. Lassell Ripley, for the loan of the original plate from the American Widgeon design which has been restruck for the special limited edition; Robert Hines, without whose invaluable help this book might never have been completed; "The Crossroads of Sport," which generously gave its time and resources and helped me immeasurably in the research of this book and lastly, the numerous artists whose work appears in these pages.

Among the written sources which supplied valuable information, I would especially like to acknowledge several government publications: *Federal Duck Stamps and Their Place in Waterfowl Conservation* by Edna Sater (Washington: U.S. Government Printing Office, 1947), *Duck Stamps and Wildlife Refuges* by John L. Farley (Washington: U.S. Government Printing Office, 1955), and *Duck Stamp Data* (Washington: U.S. Government Printing Office, 1969). Peter Matthiessen's *Wildlife in America* (New York: Viking, 1964), a superb survey of the diminution of wildlife in North America and of efforts to preserve it, provided background information.

Introduction

*W*HEN Ding Darling drew the first Migratory Bird Hunting Stamp, he could not know that he was inaugurating the most successful series in American stamp history. Duck stamps have appeared annually since 1934. The history of each stamp's creation is as interesting as its purpose. In the early years individual artists were commissioned, but by 1948 so many designs were submitted voluntarily that a contest to select the winner became a necessity. In its growth since then, the contest has helped gain recognition for wildlife art and artists. Designing the stamp is such a singular honor that it immediately confers national and international respect upon the winner.

In many ways, my two decades of work with the Duck Stamp Committee has been as rewarding as drawing the first redhead stamp, long ago now. Everyone connected with production of the annual stamp—the men in our Bureau, in the Post Office Department and in the Bureau of Engraving and Printing—has shared pride and enthusiasm in working with this series.

In *Art for Conservation*, Jene Gilmore has detailed the history of the series and accented the fact that the revenues from stamp sales are all for the birds—the restoration of waterfowl. It does not matter which of us, hunter or bird watcher, will benefit the most. What does concern us is that wildlife artists and technicians are using their skills to maintain the high aims of this unique series—to keep the flocks flying. May the artists and the ducks both flourish.

Bob Hines, CHAIRMAN, DUCK STAMP COMMITTEE
BUREAU OF SPORT FISHERIES AND WILDLIFE

Foreword

THE Migratory Bird Hunting Stamp, known informally as the duck stamp, like invention, was born of necessity. In 1934 waterfowl resources on the North American continent had declined to a critical number of both birds and habitats, and sportsmen and conservationists, formerly often antagonists, recognized a common interest in the protection and nurture of the nation's migratory waterfowl. The federal government, as the result of an agreement with Great Britain, and at the prodding of interested organizations, also had a responsibility to safeguard and manage all migratory waterfowl. Part of the resolution of the crisis was the adoption of the duck stamp, which was issued for hunting seasons throughout the states in that crucial year. The stamp succeeded in raising funds for the purchase and development of waterfowl refuges, after more than a century of legislation, organizations of sportsmen and of conservationists had failed to stop the downward spiral of migratory waterfowl toward extinction.

When the continent was undergoing the first century of exploration and settlement the variety and quantity of wildlife observed was overwhelming. To the man who stood at noon below a sky almost as dark as night with flights of passenger pigeons or who rode by thousands of square miles of grazing bison, it would have been inconceivable that the slightest species of the teeming birds and animals could pass forever from the face of the earth. The continent was incredibly rich in wildlife resources, and the shape, position and temperature of the land especially favored migratory waterfowl. Four flyways divided the continent—the Pacific, the Central, the Mississippi and the Atlantic—and each species of bird traveled the same route each year, from north to south, and back again. Along these flyways, from the northern-most edges of Canada, to destinations in the United States and Mexico, the migrating birds found immense feeding and breeding grounds. Over one-hundred-and-eighty species of gamebird

were identified in the nineteenth century, and of these, over fifty species were classed as waterfowl.

As early as the beginning of the nineteenth century, however, the effects of commercial gunning and man's domination of the wilderness were noticed. Inevitably more and more areas which fed and bred migratory birds were preempted by man, and more and more efficient guns and ammunition were manufactured. As the years passed and the number of birds noticeably lessened, various measures were adopted and groups formed to resist the steady reduction of bird life. New York State in 1838 passed a law prohibiting the use of multiple guns for the hunting of waterfowl, but gunners took to wearing disguises and threatening informers with violence. The law, a practical failure, was repealed. In 1844, The New York Association for the Protection of Game, the first organization of its kind, was formed. That year was the last when elk and wild turkey were seen in the state. Public sentiment favoring conservationist practices was growing. But sentiment and restrictive legislation by many of the states did not prevent the increasingly rapid diminution of gamebirds in the nation. Toward the end of the nineteenth century the market for edible shorebirds grew, and the birds dwindled in inverse proportion to the growing appetite for the delicacy of game. Market gunners began killing thirty or forty birds with one punt shot, and between 1870 and 1875 it was not uncommon for gunners to take 15,000 ducks in one day in the Chesapeake Bay area. Many experts predicted extinction for the majority of species of waterfowl.

In 1883 the American Ornithologist's Union was formed, naming their journal, *The Auk*, and hoping to save extant species of birds from the fate of its auspicious namesake. The AOU did arouse official interest in the plight of bird life in the country, and on March 14, 1903,

President Theodore Roosevelt established the first national wildlife refuge. Pelican Island, a three-acre mangrove-covered island in the Indian River on Florida's east coast was declared a refuge, and the rookeries of colonial birds roosting there were protected from the depredations of the millinery trade for their plumage. By 1906 there were five refuges, and their maintenance was provided by private funds, mostly from the National Audubon Society, which was allied with the AOU. By 1913, nearly 25 national wildlife refuges, containing hundreds of islands were designated for the protection of colonial birds, including several in Alaska. These refuges were the beginning of a constructive program to protect, not only birds, but other species of wildlife as well. Previously, the only method of solving the problem of declining species of wildlife had been restrictive legislation, in the form of closed seasons, which had failed to accomplish its purpose. Yet, federal laws and taxes to preserve wildlife were unpopular, and in the early 1900s, when the idea of a federal income tax was widely considered to be unconstitutional, legislative attempts to move in that direction were vetoed.

Despite the establishment of these refuges, actually less a solution than a gesture when measured against the extent of the problem, the alarming reduction of waterfowl continued. Wilderness regions were being cleared for agriculture, and wetlands were the target of vast drainage projects which rendered the land useless to waterfowl, fish and fur animals, and, ironically, as it developed, to farmers. In 1915 a long period of dwindling precipitation began over hundreds of thousands of square miles of the finest breeding areas in the north–central states and the southern part of the Prairie Provinces of Canada. The future of waterfowl had become grave enough to warrant action that eclipsed national boundaries.

In 1916 the United States entered a treaty with Great Britain, the purpose of which was to reverse the trend of migratory bird life toward extinction. The treaty stated in part:

> "...Many species of birds in the course of their annual migrations traverse certain parts of the United States and the Dominion of Canada; and...many of these species are of great value as a source of food or in destroying insects which are injurious to forests and forage plants on the public domain, as well as to agricultural crops, in both the United States and Canada, but are nevertheless in danger of extermination through lack of protection during the nesting season or while on their way to and from their breeding grounds...(the United States and Great Britain) being desirous of saving from indiscriminate slaughter and of insuring preservation of such migratory birds as are either useful to man or are harmless, have resolved to adopt some uniform system of protection..."

The system of protection consisted mainly of closed seasons to the hunting of a number of species of migratory birds.

The Migratory Bird Treaty Act was passed by Congress in 1918, and the significant effect of this agreement was to place the federal government under obligation to protect the birds identified in the agreement. Government efforts to support the treaty, and the outbreak of World War I, which drastically limited the number of hunters in the field, were responsible for a dramatic increase in the waterfowl population, and in 1921, the fall migration soared to a number of flights last observed in the early 1900s.

Soon after the war, the waterfowl population began again to drop toward a perilous low. The drought continued unabated. A variety of interests converged upon the migratory waterfowl problem in the bleak days of the late 1920s. In 1925 and 1926 a bill—H.R. 7479—was introduced into Congress. It proposed to meet the obligations of the Migratory Bird Treaty by establishing and funding bird refuges which would also serve as "Public Shooting Grounds." The bill aroused furious controversy. The American Game Protective and Propagation Association and the National Association of Audubon Societies (which contended that any increase in the duck population on the food-scarce wintering grounds would result in mass starvation), among other groups, aligned themselves in favor of the bill. Conservationists, including Aldo Leopold, sportsmen's organizations and legislators, especially Senator Fiorello LaGuardia, denounced the bill. LaGuardia took the Game Protective Association to task for representing the interests of gun and ammunition manufacturers, and summed up the position of the opposition in an address to the House of Representatives:

"I am unalterably opposed to an unsportsmanlike bill, which under the guise of a conservation of bird life bill, creates so-called sanctuaries that may be turned into shooting grounds for unsportsmen hunters to slaughter birds."

Bill H.R. 7479 did not pass.

Other, more constructive steps, were taken by private organizations. In 1929, the "More Game Birds In America Foundation" was formed. It devoted its initial efforts to surveying continental waterfowl populations and then proceeded to the job of rehabilitating and preserving primary nesting areas of geese and ducks. This group became Ducks Unlimited in 1937, and to this day, has dedicated its resources to the establishment, design and maintenance of suitable habitats for migratory waterfowl. The aims of this group prefigured the program of the Duck Stamp Act.

By the same year, 1929, the federal government had realized that caring for the waterfowl in accordance with the intent of the Migratory Bird Treaty Act meant more than protecting them from destruction by the gun. It had to take the responsibility to provide places where the birds could breed, feed, rest and find wintering grounds. In 1929 Congress passed the Migratory Bird Conservation Act, which authorized a program of acquisition of land and water areas to be used as inviolate sanctuaries for birds. The Act established the Migratory Bird Conservation Commission, composed of the Secretaries of Agriculture, Commerce and Interior and two members each from the Senate and the House. This commission was to pass on all land purchases made under the provisions of the Act. The Bureau of Biological Survey, a predecessor of the Fish and Wildlife Service, began surveys of areas throughout the United States in order to find lands suitable for purchase.

Unfortunately, governmental and private efforts to save the nation's heritage of migratory waterfowl seemed doomed to failure. The early thirties were disastrous. The drought, which had accumulated the force of two decades, was most severe. Water had disappeared from prairie ponds, from potholes and marshes; dust storms raged, and farmers throughout the Dust Bowl were impoverished. By 1934 all available records for duration, extent and severity of drought had been broken. The worst effects of the drought were felt in areas that formerly had been important breeding grounds for highly prized species of wild ducks, such as the canvasback and redhead. At the same time, the effectiveness and number of guns increased two-fold, and new and more deadly methods of hunting were introduced. Each year of the period between 1921 and 1931 saw the kill of ducks probably exceed the number that left the nesting grounds by approximately 9 million. The depredations of previous decades, the fickleness of nature and foolishness of man, all combined in 1934 to reduce the total population of ducks and geese to the critically low point of 27 million. The Depression made funds to implement the Conservation Act of 1929 as scarce as water in the deserts of the prairies. Again many conservationists predicted the early extinction of the nation's ducks and geese.

In 1934, when the need was most acute, a program for funding the care of migratory birds was proposed which would support and supplement the Migratory Bird Conservation Act of 1929. July 1, the date of the Migratory Bird Hunting Stamp—or the Duck Stamp Act—was to mark a turning point in conservation history. Six months before the enactment of the stamp program, a special committee composed of Jay N. "Ding" Darling, Thomas Beck and Aldo Leopold, appointed by President Franklin D. Roosevelt, had been working on a program for the purchase and development of lands for waterfowl and upland game refuges. They set a goal of 50 million dollars, a figure which astonished the public and inspired conservationists. Reorganization of the Bureau of Biological Survey was accomplished when the Secretary of Agriculture, Henry Wallace, prevailed upon "Ding" Darling to become Bureau Chief. In the next 15 months Darling personally obtained 16.5 million dollars for the new refuge program. He established the Refuge Division, and with labor from the WPA and CCC, gave the program a fine start. The creation and sale of duck stamps—which by 1970 had realized over 175 million dollars for migratory waterfowl refuges—was an important part of their plan.

Beck and Leopold requested that Darling design the inaugural stamp, which he did. The stamp depicted two mallards dropping onto the surface of a marsh pond. The stamps were to be sold annually, and were a federal requirement of all waterfowl hunters. The money the stamps raised was to be applied directly to the purchase and maintenance of waterfowl refuges.

The stamps gave impetus to a constructive conservation program at a time when other funds were practically unavailable. Over the years the sale of duck stamps has supplemented federal appropriations for waterfowl refuges, but many specific projects and accomplishments can be directly attributed to the stamp program. The Horicon National Wildlife Refuge near Waupan, Wisconsin, in 1940, became a 21,000 acre sanctuary mainly as a result of duck stamp funds. Fifty-two-thousand acres of the "Mysterious Okefenokee" swamp area in Georgia were designated as a national wildlife refuge. Duck stamp money made this refuge possible. Key waterfowl sanctuary areas on the Atlantic Coast purchased by duck stamp funds include the Parker River Refuge in Massachusetts, the Chincoteague Refuge in Virginia and the Brigantine Refuge in New Jersey.

The cackling goose is one of several species of migratory waterfowl which have especially benefited from the duck stamp act. A Californian in winter, the goose had been threatened by the state's extensive drainage projects. Duck stamp dollars helped to create the Sacramento Refuge and the Tule Lake Refuge, both among the favorite wintering grounds of the goose. The acquisition and development of the Red Rock Lakes refuge in Montana played an important role in saving the trumpeter swan from extinction.

These are just a very few examples of the accomplishments wrought by the duck stamp act. Waterfowl refuges have been established in 46 of the 50 states, and center on those areas which are traditionally breeding and feeding grounds of migratory birds. Purchase of land is merely the initial step in the establishment of a refuge. The birds must have food and fresh water, and other items, such as gravel, to fulfill their special living requirements. Each refuge is developed to provide maximum value to the greatest number of species, particularly during emergency periods. To provide food for the birds, the Fish and Wildlife Service has become one of the nation's largest farmers—producing such varied crops as rice, wheat, corn, barley, clovers, millets, buckwheat and maize. In addition to development, administration and enforcement of the refuges, the Service must meet the hazards of pollution and threats to the ecology of the sanctuaries from the surrounding areas.

Despite all that has been done to protect migratory waterfowl, they still face serious threats to their survival from urban and agricultural needs. The future of wildlife is and will be precarious, but duck stamps continue to perform a crucial role in conserving and preserving migratory waterfowl.

The Migratory Bird Hunting Stamp Act provides that any person over 16 years of age who hunts wild ducks, geese or brant must purchase and carry a federal stamp, signed in ink across the face. The hunter must, of course, observe the licensing laws of the state in which he hunts. Only one duck stamp is required, however, regardless of the number of states in which the sportsman hunts. Persons who collect migratory birds for scientific purposes must also have the stamp, as well as the federal scientific collecting permit. The penalty for any violation of the Duck Stamp Act is a fine of not more than $500, six months' imprisonment or both.

Until 1951 the funds derived from the Duck Stamp Act were allocated thusly: 90% to the Fish and Wildlife Service to supplement other monies for the purchase, development and maintenance of waterfowl refuges throughout the country. The remaining 10% was used for printing and distributing the stamps, and for enforcement of the Act and other federal laws regarding migratory bird conservation. In 1951 the proportion of money to be used for administration and enforcement of the Act was increased to 15%. The Post Office oversees sale of the stamps.

Several amendments to the Act over the years have changed relatively minor aspects of the program. In 1949, the price of the stamp was raised from $1 to $2, and in 1958, the price increased again to $3 in order to offset rising land costs and to meet the need to expand the waterfowl conservation work. In 1960 the Secretary of the Interior was granted by Congress the discretionary power to open portions of migratory bird refuges to the hunting of game birds.

For the first 15 years the central design of the stamp was commissioned by the committee administrating the duck stamp act. "Ding" Darling created the initial design in 1934 and Frank W. Benson and Richard E. Bishop were called upon to contribute the designs for the following two years. Beginning in 1949, the selection of art to provide the motif for the stamp shifted from commission to an annual contest, which is now open to all interested artists. The opening of the contest is announced in July by the Bureau of Sport Fisheries and Wildlife in Washington, D.C., and the judging of entries takes place in December. The competing artists can choose almost any medium in which to work—pen-and-ink, oil, watercolor, etching, pencil, etc. The sketches must be 7 inches wide and 5 inches high. The winning artist receives no compensation except an album containing a sheet of the stamp he designed, but the distinction achieved by the winner is unique. Prints and reproductions of the original art have been sold through galleries and sporting stores since the first years of the duck stamp act.

The stamp itself, quite apart from its function in waterfowl conservation, has become of considerable interest to philatelists. The finished stamp design is 1.21 inches vertical by 1.82 inches horizontal. The stamps are printed on unwatermarked paper and are perforated 11 x 11. Up to and including the 1958–59 issue, printing was performed on a four-plate flatbed power press; since then sheet-fed Giori rotary presses which carry two plates print either single color or multicolor, using from one to three inks at one passage. Issues previous to 1941 are exceedingly rare, due to the destruction of all unsold stamps after the year of issue had expired, as specified by law. After 1941, however, unsold stamps were permitted to be turned over to the Philatelic Agency of the Post Office in Washington, D.C. and "therein placed on sale until disposed of or until the Congress otherwise provides." Early issues command prices far in excess of their original cost and are available only from private collectors or stamp dealers.

1934–1935 Duck Stamp

MALLARD DUCK

DESIGN
Two mallards, a hen and a drake, landing in a windy marsh.

ARTIST
J. N. "Ding" Darling, cartoonist and conservationist, former head of the Biological Survey Bureau (a predecessor of the Fish and Wildlife Service), designed the inaugural migratory waterfowl hunting stamp.

PHILATELIC DATA
Color: Blue.
Designer: Alvin R. Meissner.
Engravers: Vignette, Carl T. Arlt; Frame, Lettering and Numerals, Frank Lamasure.
Plates Issued: 129199, 129200, 129201, 129202.
Inscribed: "U.S. Department of Agriculture. Void after June 30, 1935."
First Day of Sale: August 14, 1934.
Quantity Sold: 635,001.

Mallard Duck

1935–1936 Duck Stamp

CANVASBACK DUCK

DESIGN
Three canvasbacks in their first sweep through the air after taking off from the placid surface of a pond strewn with water plants.

ARTIST
Frank W. Benson, N.A., painter, who has been called the dean of American duck etchers. There are volumes of books depicting his paintings and etchings.

PHILATELIC DATA
Color: Rose lake.
Designer: Alvin R. Meissner.
Engravers: Vignette, Carl T. Arlt; Frame, Lettering and Numerals, Donald R. McLeod.
Plates Issued: 131980, 131981, 131982, 131983.
Inscribed: "U.S. Department of Agriculture. Void after June 30, 1936."
First Day of Sale: July 1, 1935.
Quantity Sold: 448,204.

CANVASBACK DUCK

1936–1937 Duck Stamp

CANADA GOOSE

DESIGN

Three Canada geese on the wing, against a background of cumulus clouds. (The center bird has a band on the right leg. The Fish and Wildlife Service uses numbered bands to trace the routes of migratory birds.)

ARTIST

Richard E. Bishop, an artist internationally known for his wildlife etchings on glass and china, and for his photography. Illustrated and photographed for the book *Prairie Wings* by Edgar Queeney. The first artist to actually make an etching of the duck stamp design.

PHILATELIC DATA

Color: Brown-black.

Designer: Alvin R. Meissner.

Engravers: Vignette, James R. Lowe; Frame, Lettering and Numerals, Frank Lamasure.

Plates Issued: 124317, 124318.

Inscribed: "U.S. Department of Agriculture. Void after June 30, 1937."

First Day of Sale: July 1, 1936.

Quantity Sold: 603,623.

Canada Goose

1937–1938 Duck Stamp

GREATER SCAUP DUCK

DESIGN

Three male and two female scaups, known respectively as "Bluebills" and "Broadbills," approach a feeding area off the Great South Bay, Long Island, New York. The scene is typical of waterfowl feeding grounds along the Atlantic Coast.

ARTIST

J. D. Knap, a wildlife artist, whose paintings were exhibited widely, including in the Museum of Natural History in New York City, and whose illustrations appeared in many magazines.

PHILATELIC DATA

Color: Light green.

Designer: Alvin R. Meissner.

Engravers: Vignette, James R. Lowe; Frame, Donald R. McLeod; Lettering, D. R. McLeod, William B. Wells, Alton Payne; Numerals, Alton Payne.

Plate Issued: 136267.

Inscribed: "U.S. Department of Agriculture. Void after June 30, 1938."

First Day of Sale: July 1, 1937.

Quantity Sold: 783,039.

GREATER SCAUP DUCK

1938–1939 Duck Stamp

PINTAIL DUCK

DESIGN
Pintail duck and drake coming in for a landing.

ARTIST
Roland Clark, etcher of wildlife subjects, who wrote and illustrated books on hunting—*Stray Shots* and *Gunner's Dawn*. Many of his etchings were reproduced in the book *Roland Clark's Etchings*. One of America's first great wildlife painters.

PHILATELIC DATA
Color: Light violet.
Designer: Alvin R. Meissner.
Engravers: Vignette, James R. Lowe; Frame, Donald R. McLeod; Lettering, D. R. McLeod, James T. Vail; Numerals, James T. Vail.
Plate Issued: 138602.
Inscribed: "U.S. Department of Agriculture. Void after June 30, 1939."
First Day of Sale: July 1, 1938.
Quantity Sold: 1,002,715.

Pintail Duck

1939–1940 Duck Stamp

GREEN-WING TEAL

DESIGN
A male and female teal standing at a marsh edge, with five teal in the background descending for a landing.

ARTIST
Lynn Bogue Hunt, wildlife artist and illustrator of books on nature and sport.

PHILATELIC DATA
Color: Chocolate.
Designer: William K. Schrage.
Engravers: Vignette, Matthew D. Fenton; Frame, William B. Wells; Lettering and Numerals, George K. Huber.
Plate Issued: 141428.
Inscribed: "U.S. Department of the Interior. Void after June 30, 1940."
Note: The Bureau of Biological Survey of the U.S. Department of Agriculture was transferred to the Department of the Interior by presidential order on July 1, 1939. On July 1, 1940, the Bureau of Biological Survey and the Bureau of Fisheries were merged in the Department of the Interior to form the Fish and Wildlife Service.
First Day of Sale: July 1, 1939.
Quantity Sold: 1,111,561.

Green-wing Teal

1940–1941 Duck Stamp

BLACK DUCK

DESIGN
A pair of Black ducks flying downwind over a marsh, against a background of wild rice.

ARTIST
Francis L. Jacques, whose illustrations appeared in, among other books, *Birds of Minnesota* and *Florida Bird Life*. He painted backgrounds for habitat groups in natural history museums in New York City and Minneapolis.

PHILATELIC DATA
Color: Sepia.
Designer: Victor S. McCloskey, Jr.
Engravers: Vignette, Matthew D. Fenton; Frame, Lettering and Numerals, James T. Vail.
Plates Issued: 143743, 143776.
Inscribed: "U.S. Department of the Interior. Void after June 30, 1941."
First Day of Sale: July 1, 1940.
Quantity Sold: 1,260,810.

BLACK DUCK

1941–1942 Duck Stamp

RUDDY DUCK

DESIGN

A male and female ruddy duck with their brood swimming at the edge of a marsh.

ARTIST

E. R. Kalmbach, painter of wildlife subjects, ornithologist, mammalogist and former head of the Fish and Wildlife Service's research laboratory at Denver, Colorado.

PHILATELIC DATA

Color: Brown carmine.

Designer: Victor S. McCloskey, Jr.

Engravers: Vignette, Charles A. Brooks; Frame, Lettering and Numerals, Axel W. Christensen.

Plates Issued: 146271, 146282.

Inscribed: "U.S. Department of the Interior. Void after June 30, 1942."

First Day of Sale: July 1, 1941.

Quantity Sold: 1,439,967.

Ruddy Duck

1942–1943 Duck Stamp

WIDGEON, OR BALDPATE DUCK

DESIGN
A pair of widgeons by a coastal marsh awaiting a descending drake.

ARTIST
A. Lassell Ripley, wildlife etcher, watercolorist and painter whose work appeared in the Boston Museum of Fine Arts and The Chicago Art Institute, among other museums and galleries. Included in his honors was election to the National Academy of Design.

PHILATELIC DATA
Color: Brown.
Designer: William K. Schrage.
Engravers: Vignette, Carl T. Arlt; Outline, Frame, Lettering and Numerals, George L. Huber.
Plates Issued: 149599, 149600.
Inscribed: "U.S. Department of the Interior. Void after June 30, 1943."
First Day of Sale: July 1, 1942.
Quantity Sold: 1,383,629.

WIDGEON, OR BALDPATE DUCK

1943–1944 Duck Stamp

WOOD DUCK

DESIGN
Two wood ducks in flight.

ARTIST
Walter E. Bohl, several of whose etchings are in a permanent collection in the National Gallery of Art at Washington, D.C.

PHILATELIC DATA
Color: Indian red.
Designer: Victor S. McCloskey, Jr.
Engravers: Vignette, Charles A. Brooks; Outline, Frame, Lettering and Numerals, John S. Edmondson.
Plates Issued: 152826, 152827.
Inscribed: "U.S. Department of the Interior. Void after June 30, 1944."
First Day of Sale: July 1, 1943.
Quantity Sold: 1,169,352.

Wood Duck

1944–1945 Duck Stamp

WHITE-FRONTED GOOSE

DESIGN
Three white-fronted geese, part of a flock, coming in.

ARTIST
Walter A. Weber, formerly chief scientific illustrator with the National Park Service, contributed art work to *National Geographic* magazine, *Birds of Minnesota*, *Fading Trails*, *Meeting the Mammals* and *Wolves of North America*. Many of the Wildlife Conservation Stamps issued annually by the National Wildlife Federation were created by him.

PHILATELIC DATA
Color: Red-orange.
Designer: William K. Schrage.
Engravers: Vignette, Matthew D. Fenton; Frame, Lettering and Numerals, George L. Huber.
Plates Issued: 155590, 155603.
Inscribed: "U.S. Department of the Interior. Void after June 30, 1945."
First Day of Sale: July 1, 1944.
Quantity Sold: 1,487,029.

White-fronted Goose

1945–1946 Duck Stamp

SHOVELLER DUCK

DESIGN
A female and male shovellers or "spoonbills" in flight.

ARTIST
Owen J. Gromme, curator of birds and mammals at the Milwaukee Public Museum, one of the outstanding wildlife artists of the century. He wrote and illustrated *Birds of Wisconsin,* and his paintings have been exhibited widely in museums and acquired by private collectors.

PHILATELIC DATA
Color: Black and white.
Designer: Victor S. McCloskey, Jr.
Engravers: Vignette, Matthew D. Fenton; Outline, Frame, Lettering and Numerals, John S. Edmondson.
Plates Issued: 157248, 157249.
Inscribed: "U.S. Department of the Interior. Void after June 30, 1946."
First Day of Sale: July 1, 1945.
Quantity Sold: 1,725,505.

SHOVELLER DUCK

1946–1947 Duck Stamp

REDHEAD DUCK

DESIGN
A female and three male redheads riding the water, and another male alighting.

ARTIST
Robert W. Hines wrote and illustrated *Ducks At A Distance* and illustrated Rachel Carson's *The Edge of the Sea,* Peter Matthiessen's *Wildlife in America,* and Peter Farb's *Face of North America,* to name a few of the books containing his work. His illustrations have appeared in numerous magazines, including *Natural History, Sports Afield,* and the *New Yorker.* He designed the first four stamps in the Wildlife Conservation Postage Stamp Series.

PHILATELIC DATA
Color: Medium dark maroon-brown.
Designer: William K. Schrage.
Engravers: Vignette, Matthew D. Fenton; Lettering, Frame and Numerals, John S. Edmondson.
Plates Issued: 158448, 158449, 158456, 158457; back plate 47510 (offset).
Inscribed: "U.S. Department of the Interior. Void after June 30, 1947."
First Day of Sale: July 1, 1946.
Quantity Sold: 2,016,819.

REDHEAD DUCK

1947–1948 Duck Stamp

SNOW GOOSE

DESIGN
Two snow geese in flight.

ARTIST
Jack Murray, a painter of wildlife whose work appeared on the cover of the *Saturday Evening Post* and in the pages of a host of national magazines. He illustrated nature subjects for the American Museum of Natural History in New York City.

PHILATELIC DATA
Color: Black on white.
Designer: Victor S. McCloskey, Jr.
Engravers: Vignette, Arthur Dintaman; Frame, Lettering and Numerals, Axel W. Christensen.
Plates Issued: 159461, 159462, 159463, 159464, back plate 47510.
Inscribed: "U.S. Department of the Interior. Void after June 30, 1948."
First Day of Sale: July 1, 1947.
Quantity Sold: 1,722,677.

SNOW GOOSE

1948–1949 Duck Stamp

BUFFLE-HEAD DUCK

DESIGN
Three buffle-heads, two male and a female, in flight.

ARTIST
Maynard Reece, sportsman and artist, whose paintings have been exhibited in galleries and museums all over the country; his illustrations have appeared in *Life* and *Sports Illustrated*, among other magazines, and he wrote and illustrated the book *Fish and Fishing*. The only five time winner in this outstanding contest.

PHILATELIC DATA
Color: Brilliant light blue.
Designers: Central Design by Maynard Reece; Frame and Lettering by Robert L. Miller, Jr.
Engravers: Vignette, Arthur W. Dintaman; Frame, Lettering and Numerals, Axel W. Christensen.
Plates Issued: 160099, 160100, 160101, 160102, back plate 47510.
Inscribed: "U.S. Department of the Interior. Void after June 30, 1949."
First Day of Sale: July 1, 1948.
Quantity Sold: 2,127,603.

BUFFLE-HEAD DUCK

1949–1950 Duck Stamp

GOLDENEYE DUCK

DESIGN

A male and a female goldeneye wing over a quiet cove on which several other goldeneyes are performing courtship displays.

ARTIST

Roger E. Preuss, artist and decoy designer. Youngest artist to ever win the design. Avid conservationist and director of Wetlands for Wildlife. His paintings are exhibited in some of the finest collections.

PHILATELIC DATA

Color: Brilliant green.

Designers: Central design by Roger E. Preuss; Frame and Lettering by Robert L. Miller.

Engravers: Vignette, Richard M. Bower; Frame, Lettering and Numerals, John S. Edmondson.

Plates Issued: 160790, 160791, 160792, 160793, back plate 47510.

Inscribed: "U.S. Department of the Interior. Void after June 30, 1950. $2."

First Day of Sale: September 1, 1949.

Quantity Sold: 1,954,734.

GOLDENEYE DUCK

1950–1951 Duck Stamp

TRUMPETER SWAN

DESIGN
The original black-and-white wash drawing depicts two trumpeter swans flying over the Red Rock Lakes National Wildlife Refuge in Montana.

ARTIST
Walter A. Weber (also winner of the 1944–45 duck stamp competition).

PHILATELIC DATA
Color: Brilliant purplish blue.
Designers: Central design by Walter A. Weber. Frame and Lettering by Victor S. McCloskey, Jr.
Engravers: Vignette, Arthur A. Dintaman; Frame, Lettering and Numerals, Reuben K. Barrick.
Plates Issued: 161533, 161534, 161535, 161536, back plate 47510.
Inscribed: "U.S. Department of the Interior. Void after June 30, 1951. $2."
First Day of Sale: July 1, 1950.
Quantity Sold: 1,903,644.

TRUMPETER SWAN

1951–1952 Duck Stamp

GADWALL DUCK

DESIGN
Two gadwall ducks rising from a pond.

ARTIST
Maynard Reece (also winner of the 1948–49 duck stamp competition).

PHILATELIC DATA
Color: Smoke gray.
Designers: Central design by Maynard Reece; Frame and Lettering by William K. Schrage.
Engravers: Vignette, Richard M. Bower; Outline, Frame, Lettering and Numerals, Reuben K. Barrick.
Plates Issued: 162125, 162126, 162127, 162128, back plate 47510.
Inscribed: "U.S. Department of the Interior. Void after June 30, 1952. $2."
First Day of Sale: July 1, 1951.
Quantity Sold: 2,167,767.

GADWALL DUCK

1952–1953 Duck Stamp

HARLEQUIN DUCK

DESIGN
The original black-and-white wash drawing depicts a harlequin drake and hen flying against high waves.

ARTIST
John H. Dick, a photographer and artist who specializes in bird subjects. His illustrations appear in Olin Pettingill's *The Bird Watchers of America* and H. M. Hall's *A Gathering of Shore Birds,* to name a few of the books containing his art.

PHILATELIC DATA
Color: Lilac blue.
Designers: Central design by John H. Dick; Frame and Lettering by Robert L. Miller, who also added necessary detail to the central design to make it suitable for bank note engraving.
Engravers: Vignette, George A. Gundersen; Frame, Lettering and Numerals, John S. Edmondson.
Plate Numbers: 162602, 162603, 162604, 162605, back plate 47510.
Inscribed: "U.S. Department of the Interior. Void after June 30, 1952. $2. Harlequin Ducks." (This is the first duck stamp to have the name of the species imprinted on it.)
First Day of Sale: July 1, 1952.
Quantity Sold: 2,296,628.

Harlequin Duck

1953–1954 Duck Stamp

BLUE-WINGED TEAL

DESIGN
Five blue-winged teal in flight over bulrush. The original sketch, a black-and-white wash drawing, is entitled "Early Express."

ARTIST
Clayton B. Seagears, conservationist and artist. He founded the magazine *The Conservationist*, and his illustrations have graced the pages of *Field and Stream*, *Outdoors Unlimited* and *The Saturday Evening Post*, among others.

PHILATELIC DATA
Color: Maroon.
Designers: Central design by Clayton B. Seagears; Frame and Lettering by William K. Schrage.
Engravers: Vignette, Arthur W. Dintaman; Frame, Lettering and Numerals, Robert J. Jones.
Plate Numbers: 163622, 163623, 163624, 163625, back plate 47510.
Inscribed: "U.S. Department of the Interior. Void after June 30, 1954. $2. Blue-Winged Teal."
First Day of Sale: July 1, 1953.
Quantity Sold: 2,268,446.

BLUE-WINGED TEAL

1954–1955 Duck Stamp

RING-NECKED DUCK

DESIGN

The original black-and-white watercolor shows a ring-neck drake and hen slanting in for a landing.

ARTIST

Harvey D. Sandstrom, sportsman and artist, whose work has been shown in many galleries in New York, Chicago and other cities across the country.

PHILATELIC DATA

Color: Black and white.

Designers: Central design by Harvey D. Sandstrom; Frame and Lettering by Victor S. McCloskey, Jr.

Engravers: Vignette, Matthew D. Fenton; Frame, Lettering and Numerals, George L. Huber.

Plate Numbers: 164744, 164745, 164746, 164747, back plate 52412.

Inscribed: "U.S. Department of the Interior. Void after June 30, 1955. $2. Ring-necked Duck."

First Day of Sale: July 1, 1954.

Quantity Sold: 2,184,550.

RING-NECKED DUCK

1955–1956 Duck Stamp

BLUE GEESE

DESIGN
Three blue geese pass over a cattail marsh. The original sketch is a black-and-white opaque watercolor.

ARTIST
Stanley Stearns, an artist known for his oils, etchings and watercolors, as well as illustrations. His work appears in many public and private collections.

PHILATELIC DATA
Color: Medium dark blue.
Designers: Central design by Stanley Stearns, Frame and Lettering by Robert L. Miller.
Engravers: Vignette, Richard M. Bower; Frame, Lettering and Numerals, Robert J. Jones.
Plate Numbers: 165282, 165283, 165284, 165285, back plate 52412.
Inscribed: "U.S. Department of the Interior. Void after June 30, 1956. $2. Blue Geese."
First Day of Sale: July 1, 1955.
Quantity Sold: 2,369,940.

BLUE GEESE

1956–1957 Duck Stamp

AMERICAN MERGANSER

DESIGN

A pair of American mergansers flying low over fog-bound water. The original sketch is a black-and-white watercolor.

ARTIST

Edward J. Bierly, painter of birds and animals, whose work has appeared in state and wildlife publications as well as books. He designed nature exhibits for the National Park Service.

PHILATELIC DATA

Color: Blue-black.

Designers: Central design by Edward J. Bierly, Frame and Lettering by William K. Schrage.

Engravers: Vignette, Richard M. Bower; Frame, Lettering and Numerals, George A. Payne.

Plate Numbers: 165826, 165827, 165829; 165860 for face printing; offset plate 52412 for back printing.

Inscribed: "U.S. Department of the Interior. Void after June 30, 1957. $2. American Merganser."

First Day of Sale: July 1, 1956.

Quantity Sold: 2,332,014.

American Merganser

1957–1958 Duck Stamp

AMERICAN EIDER DUCK

DESIGN

A tempera watercolor depicting two American eider ducks flying over the surf.

ARTIST

Jackson Miles Abbott, a painter and illustrator, notably of the book *Beginner's Guide to Attracting Birds*, has a particular interest in ornithology and is a member of the Audubon Society and the Virginia Society of Ornithology.

PHILATELIC DATA

Color: Medium yellowish-green.

Designers: Central design by Jackson Miles Abbott, Frame and Lettering by Victor S. McCloskey, Jr.

Engravers: Vignette, Arthur W. Dintaman; Frame, Lettering and Numerals, Howard F. Sharpless.

Plate Numbers: 166256, 166257, 166258; 166259 for face printing; offset plate 52412 for back printing.

Inscribed: "U.S. Department of the Interior. Void after June 30, 1958. $2. American Eider."

First Day of Sale: July 1, 1957.

Quantity Sold: 2,355,353.

American Eider Duck

1958–1959 Duck Stamp

CANADA GOOSE

DESIGN
Several Canada geese feeding in a picked cornfield in the upper Midwest. The original art is a black-and-white wash drawing.

ARTIST
Leslie C. Kouba, painter and illustrator, and director of the American Wildlife Art Galleries.

PHILATELIC DATA
Color: Midnight black.
Designers: Central design by Leslie C. Kouba, Frame and Lettering by Robert L. Miller.
Engravers: Vignette, Matthew D. Fenton; Frame, Lettering and Numerals, George L. Huber.
Plate Numbers: 166753, 166754, 166755; 166756 for face printing; offset plate 53752 for back printing.
Inscribed: "U.S. Department of the Interior. Void after June 30, 1959. $2. Canada Geese."
First Day of Sale: July 1, 1958.
Quantity Sold: 2,165,562.

Canada Goose

1959–1960 Duck Stamp

LABRADOR RETRIEVER WITH MALLARD DUCK

DESIGN

The original black-and-white wash drawing shows a Labrador retriever carrying a mallard drake.

ARTIST

Maynard Reece. (Also winner of the design competitions in 1948–49 and 1951–52.)

PHILATELIC DATA

Colors: Black, blue and yellow. (This stamp is the first in the series to have multi-color.)

Designers: Central design by Maynard Reece; Frame and Lettering by Bob Hines; Model by Victor S. McCloskey, Jr.

Engravers: Vignette, Arthur W. Dintaman; Frame, Lettering and Numerals, Howard F. Sharpless.

Plate Numbers: 167109 and 167120 for face printing. They originated from flat master plate 167097. Offset plate 54204 for back printing. Each of these plates contains 120 individual subjects.

Inscribed: "U.S. Department of the Interior. Void after June 30, 1960. $3. Retrievers Save Game."

First Day of Sale: July 1, 1959.

Quantity Sold: 1,628,365.

LABRADOR RETRIEVER WITH MALLARD

1960–1961 Duck Stamp

REDHEAD DUCK

DESIGN
Six redheads—a drake, a hen and four ducklings—swimming in the reeds. The original sketch is a black-and-white wash drawing.

ARTIST
John A. Ruthven, naturalist and artist specializing in wildlife, co-author of the field guide to North American waterfowl, *Top Flight*. He belongs to many art and ornithological associations, including the Society of Animal Artists in New York City and the National Audubon Society.

PHILATELIC DATA
Colors: Burnished gold, crimson brown and bonnie blue.
Designers: Central design by John A. Ruthven; Lettering by Robert L. Miller.
Engravers: Vignette, Charles A. Brooks; Lettering and Numerals, George A. Payne.
Plate Numbers: 167498 and 167503 for face printing. Offset plate 54204 for back printing. Each of these plates contains 120 individual subjects.
Inscribed: "U.S. Department of the Interior. Void after June 30, 1961. $3. Wildlife Needs Water: Preserve Wetlands. Redhead Ducks."
First Day of Sale: July 1, 1960.
Quantity Sold: 1,727,534.

REDHEAD DUCK

1961–1962 Duck Stamp

MALLARD DUCK

DESIGN
The original black-and-white wash drawing shows a mallard hen and eight ducklings in a natural habitat.

ARTIST
Edward A. Morris, a wildlife illustrator who has contributed to numerous magazines and a painter whose work has been exhibited by the American Watercolor Society as well as by galleries and museums.

PHILATELIC DATA
Colors: Dark reddish brown, yellowish brown and light blue.
Designers: Central design by Edward A. Morris; Lettering and Numerals by Victor S. McCloskey, Jr.
Engravers: Vignette, Richard M. Bower; Lettering and Numerals, Howard F. Sharpless.
Plate Numbers: 167768 and 167772 for face printing. Offset plate 55048 for back printing. Each of these plates contains 120 individual subjects.
Inscribed: "U.S. Department of the Interior. Void after June 30, 1962. Migratory Bird Hunting Stamp. $3. Mallard brood. Habitat Produces Ducks."
First Day of Sale: July 1, 1961.
Quantity Sold: 1,346,003.

Mallard Duck

1962–1963 Duck Stamp

PINTAIL DUCK

DESIGN

Two pintail drakes alighting. The original sketch is a black-and-white wash drawing.

ARTIST

Edward A. Morris. (Also designer of the stamp for 1961–62.)

PHILATELIC DATA

Colors: Grayish black, light purplish blue and moderate reddish brown.

Designers: Central design by Edward A. Morris; Frame, Lettering and Numerals by Robert L. Miller.

Engravers: Vignette, Richard M. Bower; Frame, Lettering and Numerals, William R. Burnell.

Plate Numbers: 168073 for face printing. Offset plate 55048 for back printing. Each of these plates contains 120 individual subjects.

Inscribed: "U.S. Department of the Interior. Void after June 30, 1963. Migratory Bird Hunting Stamp, $3. Pintails."

First Day of Sale: July 1, 1962.

Quantity Sold: 1,147,553.

Pintail Duck

1963–1964 Duck Stamp

BRANT

DESIGN
The original black-and-white wash drawing features two brant coming in for a landing in Atlantic coastal waters.

ARTIST
Edward J. Bierly. (Also the designer of the stamp in 1956–57.)

PHILATELIC DATA
Colors: Pale blue, moderate orange yellow and black.
Designers: Central design, Edward J. Bierly; Frame, Lettering and Numerals, William K. Schrage.
Engravers: Vignette, Charles A. Brooks; Frame, Lettering and Numerals, William R. Burnell.
Plate Numbers: 168269 and 168273 for face printing. Offset plate 55048 for back printing. Each of these plates contains 120 individual subjects.
Inscribed: "U.S. Department of the Interior. Void after June 30, 1964. Migratory Bird Hunting Stamp, $3. Brant."
First Day of Sale: July 1, 1963.
Quantity Sold: 1,455,486.

BRANT

1964–1965 Duck Stamp

NENE GOOSE

DESIGN
Two nene geese among lava flows in their Hawaiian home. The original sketch is a black-and-white tempera drawing.

ARTIST
Stanley Stearns. (Also designer of the stamp in 1955–56.)

PHILATELIC DATA
Colors: Cerulean blue, khaki yellow and bluish black.

Designers: Central design, Stanley Stearns; Frame, Lettering and Numerals, Robert L. Miller.

Engravers: Vignette, Arthur W. Dintaman; Lettering and Numerals, William R. Burnell.

Plate Numbers: 168629 and 168630 for face printing. Offset plate 55048 for back printing. Each of these plates contains 120 individual subjects.

Inscribed: "U.S. Department of the Interior. Void after June 30, 1965. Migratory Bird Hunting Stamp, $3. Nene Geese."

First Day of Sale: July 1, 1964.

Quantity Sold: 1,565,860.

Nene Goose

1965–1966 Duck Stamp

CANVASBACK DUCK

DESIGN
Three canvasback drakes winging over open water. The original sketch is a black-and-white wash drawing.

ARTIST
Ron Jenkins, a lithographer and painter, with a special interest in bird subjects, whose work has appeared in the *National Geographic*, among other magazines, and is in private collections.

PHILATELIC DATA
Colors: Two different shades of brown and green.
Designers: Central design, Ron Jenkins; Lettering and Numerals, Robert L. Miller; Model, Robert L. Miller.
Engravers: Vignette, Joseph C. Creamer, Jr.; Lettering, Howard F. Sharpless.
Plate Numbers: 168790 and 168791 for face printing. Offset plate 55408 for back printing. Each of these plates contains 120 individual subjects.
Inscribed: "U.S. Department of the Interior. Void after June 30, 1966. Migratory Bird Hunting Stamp $3. Canvasbacks."
First Day of Sale: July 1, 1965.
Quantity Sold: 1,558,755.

CANVASBACK DUCK

1966–1967 Duck Stamp

WHISTLING SWAN

DESIGN
Two whistling swans fly low over a northern lake. The original sketch is a black-and-white wash drawing.

ARTIST
Stanley Stearns. (Also the designer of stamps in 1955–56 and 1964–65.)

PHILATELIC DATA
Colors: Black, blue and green.

Designers: Central design, Stanley Stearns; Lettering and Numerals, Howard C. Mildner; Model, Howard C. Mildner.

Engravers: Vignette, Charles A. Brooks; Lettering, William R. Burnell and Howard F. Sharpless.

Plate Numbers: 169058 and 169063 for face printing. Offset plate 55048 for back printing. Each of these plates contains 120 individual subjects.

Inscribed: "U.S. Department of the Interior. Void after June 30, 1967. Migratory Bird Hunting Stamp $3. Whistling Swans."

First Day of Sale: July 1, 1966.

Quantity Sold: 1,804,783.

WHISTLING SWAN

1967–1968 Duck Stamp

OLD SQUAW DUCK

DESIGN
A pair of old squaw ducks resting on a northern ice floe.

ARTIST
Leslie C. Kouba. (Also winner of the stamp competition in 1958–59.)

PHILATELIC DATA

Colors: Blue, brown and yellow.

Designers: Central design, Leslie C. Kouba; Lettering and Numerals, Robert J. Jones; Model, Robert J. Jones.

Engravers: Vignette, Edward R. Felver; Lettering, William R. Burnell.

Plate Numbers: 169457 and 169487 for face printing. Offset plate 55048 for back printing. Each of these plates contains 120 individual subjects.

Inscribed: "U.S. Department of the Interior. Void after June 30, 1968. Migratory Bird Hunting Stamp $3. Old Squaw Ducks."

First Day of Sale: July 1, 1967.

Quantity Sold: 1,934,697.

OLD SQUAW DUCK

1968–1969 Duck Stamp

HOODED MERGANSER

DESIGN
Two hooded mergansers sitting on a log.

ARTIST
C. G. Pritchard, Staff Artist of the Nebraska Game and Parks Commission, as well as contributor of illustrations to Paul Johnsgard's *Animal Behavior* and Hall and Kelson's *Mammals of North America*, among other books. He has shown in museums and galleries in the East and Midwest.

PHILATELIC DATA
Colors: Black, brown and green.
Designers: Central design, C. G. Pritchard; Lettering and Numerals, Leonard E. Buckley; Model, Leonard E. Buckley.
Engravers: Vignette, Arthur W. Dintaman; Lettering, Robert G. Culin.
Plate Numbers: 170436 and 170443 for face printing. 57501 for back printing.
Inscribed: "U.S. Department of the Interior. Void after June 30, 1969. Migratory Bird Hunting Stamp $3. Hooded Merganser."
First Day of Sale: July 1, 1968.
Quantity Sold: 1,811,754.

Hooded Merganser

1969–1970 Duck Stamp

WHITE-WINGED SCOTER

DESIGN
Two white-winged scoters rise from the water.

ARTIST
Maynard Reece. (Also the designer of stamps in 1948–49, 1951–52 and 1959–60.)

PHILATELIC DATA
Colors: Brown, red, blue and black.

Designers: Central design, Maynard Reece; Lettering and Numerals, Howard C. Mildner; Model, Howard C. Mildner.

Engravers: Vignette, Edward R. Felver; Lettering, Albert Saavedra.

Plate Numbers: 170765 and 170767 for face printing. 58026 for back printing.

Inscribed: "U.S. Department of the Interior. Void after June 30, 1970. Migratory Bird Hunting Stamp $3. White-winged scoters."

First Day of Sale: July 1, 1969.

Quantity Sold: 2,087,115.

WHITE-WINGED SCOTER

1970–1971 Duck Stamp

ROSS GOOSE

DESIGN
Two Ross geese preening. The original wash drawing was the first in the stamp series to be printed in full color.

ARTIST
Edward Bierly. (Also the designer of stamps in 1956–57 and 1963–64.)

PHILATELIC DATA
Colors: Yellow, red, blue and black.
Designers: Central design, Edward Bierly; Lettering, Numerals, Model and Back Model, Leonard E. Buckley.
Engravers: Vignette and Lettering, Robert G. Culin; Engraver, Joseph S. Creamer.
Plate Numbers: Master plate, 171151; Alto numbers, 171165, 171169.
Inscribed: "U.S. Department of the Interior. Void after June 30, 1971. Migratory Bird Hunting Stamp. $3. Ross Geese."
First Day of Sale: July 1, 1970.
Quantity Sold: 3,200,000.

Ross Goose

1971–1972 Duck Stamp

CINNAMON TEAL

DESIGN
Three cinnamon teal alighting on a marsh pond.

ARTIST
Maynard Reece. (Also the designer of the stamp in the years 1948–49, 1951–52, 1959–60 and 1969–70.)

PHILATELIC DATA
Colors: Yellow, blue, green and brown.
Designers: Central design, Maynard Reece; Lettering, Numerals and Model, Leonard E. Buckley.
Engravers: Vignette and Lettering, Robert G. Culin; Engraver, Edward R. Felver.
Plate Numbers: 171586, 171587.
Inscribed: "U.S. Department of the Interior. Void after June 30, 1972. Migratory Bird Hunting Stamp. $3. Cinnamon Teal."
First Day of Sale: July 1, 1971.

Cinnamon Teal